everyday STEM

ENGINEERING

CHEMICAL ENGINEERING

Engineering is all around you

KINGFISHER
LONDON & NEW YORK

First published 2023 in the United States
by Kingfisher
120 Broadway, New York, NY 10271
Kingfisher is an imprint of
Macmillan Children's Books, London

ISBN 978-0-7534-7825-7

Distributed in the U.S. and Canada by Macmillan,
120 Broadway, New York, NY 10271

Library of Congress Cataloging-in-Publication data has been applied for.

Author: Jenny Jacoby
Illustrator: Luna Valentine
Series editor: Lizzie Davey
Series design: Jim Green

Kingfisher Books are available for special promotions and premiums.
For details contact:
Special Markets Department, Macmillan
120 Broadway, New York, NY 10271.

For more information please visit:
www.kingfisherbooks.com

Printed in China
2 4 6 8 9 7 5 3 1
1TR/1122/UG/WKT/128MA

EU representative: 1st Floor, The Liffey Trust Centre
117-126 Sheriff Street Upper, Dublin 1 D01 YC43

CONTENTS

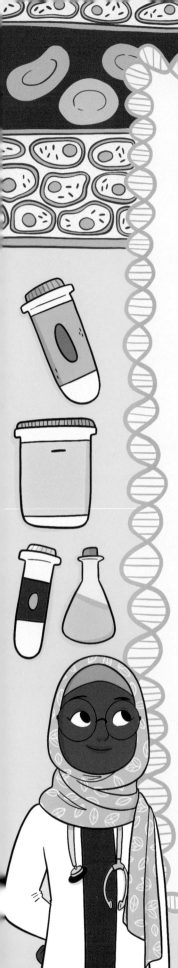

CHEMICAL ENGINEERS

Engineers are people who invent useful tools to solve problems and improve lives. They mix their knowledge of science with their creativity to spot something that could be made better and find a way to fix it. Chemical engineers work with chemicals to make useful substances to do all kinds of different jobs—from cleaning products and fuel for cars, to fertilizer to help plants grow and ways to recycle waste efficiently. This also means designing the equipment and factories needed to produce the substances.

Developing **medicines** and other useful chemicals takes a lot of trying things out, testing, and trying again to make sure they are perfectly safe for people to use.

Disinfectants are chemicals that make surfaces safe by killing microorganisms that could cause diseases, such as bacteria and molds.

Detergents are chemicals that help water wash dirty things. Chemical engineers design detergents to suit different jobs. Glass cleaner contains a detergent to remove dirt, and alcohol to help glass shine.

Chemical engineers make **fuel**. Long-distance trucks need different fuel than elite race cars or passenger jets do. Engineers also develop more environmentally friendly options, such as biofuels, which are made from renewable plant sources.

BIOMEDICAL ENGINEERS

Biomedical engineers work to help people live healthier, longer, and happier lives. They make tools that can be used by health workers in homes and hospitals, and by people at home to improve their health and lifestyle.

Genetic engineering uses chemicals to change part of a cell's genetic code, or DNA. By changing the code, the gene will do a slightly different job. This could help a body mend itself after disease, or stop a bacterium from being harmful.

Tissue engineers combine cells and other biological material with physical frames to create new body parts that can do the job of natural tissues. This technology is still developing but could help repair body parts that have been damaged.

Medical imaging machines, or scanners, show the inside of the body without damaging or hurting the patient.

Bionanotechnology is engineering with tiny biological building blocks. Using these tiny molecules, a patient can be given medicine right where it's needed, so it mends only the cells that need it.

Making **biomaterials** is a way of giving a body a new piece of equipment that can help it do its job better. Contact lenses help eyes see better, pacemakers help hearts keep rhythm, and even Band-Aids help wounds heal safely.

Prosthetics are artificial body parts that are made to replace a missing part—such as a leg or hand. Engineers are always striving to make prosthetics more comfortable and more useful.

HOW TO BE AN ENGINEER

Engineers use many different skills to come up with their inventions. Some of those skills are developed over years of study, learning the science about how the world works. Others are skills you already have and can play with all through your life: imagination, paying attention, teamwork—and a bit of luck!

No invention works perfectly the first time. By testing, tweaking, improving, and trying again, little by little, inventions can eventually be made to work smoothly and safely. They might even end up better than you first imagined!

Generations of scientists have discovered so much about the world. There is a lot of useful information to learn that will help you bring inventions to life.

Teamwork is important because everybody has different skills, so bringing different people together is much more powerful than one person working alone.

You may need to learn technical skills to engineer the invention you have imagined.

Paying attention to things big and small around you can spark ideas. Asking questions like "How does that work?" and "Could we use that idea to solve a different problem?" can help you come up with ideas for new inventions.

Imagination is very important! You have to be able to imagine a better world, or a new tool, before you can bring it to life.

SIR ALEXANDER FLEMING (1881–1955)

Fleming was born in Scotland. He studied in London, England, and worked as a medical researcher and lecturer until World War I, when he served as a captain in the British Royal Army Medical Corps.

Working in field hospitals, Fleming noticed that antiseptic wipes caused more deaths than wounds did. He realized the wipes killed germs on the skin—including helpful bacteria—but couldn't kill germs deep in the wounds.

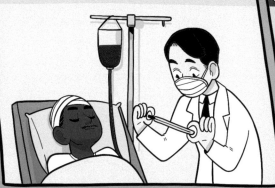

After the war Fleming returned to London, where he researched substances that could kill bacteria but not harm living cells.

In 1928, Fleming went on vacation and left a stack of Petri dishes growing bacteria on the corner of his bench. His lab was not very tidy, and drafts blew in from the hot, dirty London streets.

When he returned, Fleming saw that one of the dishes had been contaminated by a mold, and there was a ring where the mold had killed bacteria. He realized that this substance could kill the bacteria that cause disease, and named it penicillin.

Fleming moved on to other work, but in 1938 two British scientists (Howard Florey and Ernst Chain) began work on turning the mold into an antibiotic medicine. During World War II, Florey and Chain took their work to the United States.

By 1944, penicillin was being brought to the Allied soldiers fighting in Europe. At least 100,000 wounded Allied soldiers were treated with penicillin.

FROM THE LAB TO REAL LIFE

It's not easy to see chemical and biomedical engineers at work, because they usually develop their ideas in laboratories and offices. Their products might be made in factories, but even if you see shiny pipes and puffing chimneys at large factory buildings, you can't see what's going on inside them. However, what you can see for yourself is the many products created by these engineers that are part of our daily lives, and which we couldn't do without.

Bakery

It's chemistry that helps bread and cakes rise. Cake mixture includes a raising agent such as baking powder or baking soda. When these chemicals are heated in the oven, they react with other chemicals in the mixture and produce the gas carbon dioxide. Trapped inside the uncooked mixture, the gas expands, causing bubbles to grow, which make the cakes light and fluffy as they bake.

Hairdresser

Hairdressers use careful combinations of chemicals to dye hair. Ammonia hydroxide in the dye makes strands of hair puff up, creating little openings all along the hair. The molecules of color enter the hairs through these holes. Once inside, the color molecules puff up so much that they can't get out again, and the hair is dyed permanently.

Café

Chemistry helps make drinks fizzy and milk frothy! Sodas contain carbon dioxide dissolved into liquid. When the can or bottle is opened, gas escapes, making bubbles. When steam is added to milk, it becomes frothy because proteins in the milk surround air bubbles in the steam, stopping them from bursting.

Health clinics

Biomedical engineers design tools to help health-care workers care for patients and to keep people safe and healthy. They engineer ways to keep needles and syringes sterile, special materials used in face masks, and crutches and "boots" that protect damaged ankles while still allowing the patient to walk around.

Pharmacy

Different medicines in the pharmacy come in different packaging—from pills in a blister pack and thick liquid in a bottle to injections in a syringe and patches you can put on your skin. Biomedical engineers find the best way to get the medicine into you without harming any other parts of your body, helping you feel better as quickly as possible.

Swimming pool

To keep swimming pools clean and safe, chemicals such as chlorine are added to the pool water. Just the right amount of chemicals will kill off the germs that swimmers bring in, without hurting them as they swim.

THE CHEMISTRY OF WATER

We use water for washing, but water is not actually very good at getting things clean. It's not even very good at getting things wet! Have you noticed that when you put water on the back of your hand it stays in a droplet rather than spreading out? This is because it has strong surface tension—the water's surface holds itself together, like a skin. You can see water's surface tension in action on this pond.

LOW DENSITY

The rubber duck is much larger than a water strider, but it still floats on top of the water because it has a flat bottom and is filled with air. Its density is low enough that the water's surface tension can hold it up.

WIDE LOAD

Water striders spread their weight over a wide area, using six legs. They are light enough that the water's surface tension holds them up.

RESISTANCE

Water doesn't soak into leaves—it forms droplets that can easily run off a sloped surface.

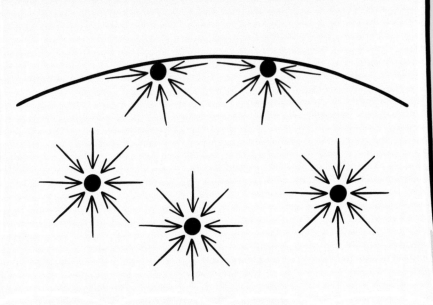

SPLASH!

When water splashes, it forms droplets. Each droplet is a spherical shape, because the surface tension pulls it together into the simplest shape possible. The smallest droplets are the roundest, because they have the strongest surface tension.

HOW DOES SURFACE TENSION WORK?

In a liquid, molecules move freely about in all directions, rubbing past each other easily. Meanwhile, a force called cohesion keeps them together. At the liquid's surface, the molecules can move in any direction, except for up. This means the cohesion pulls the molecules even closer together at the surface than they would be elsewhere. This stronger force means the water is stronger at its surface.

CLEANING WITH CHEMICALS

To clean things properly, we need to first get things wet, which means breaking down water's surface tension. This allows water molecules to reach dirt and then remove it. To do this, we use chemicals called surfactants, which reduce water's surface tension. Mixed with a surfactant, water can soak into things more easily and make bubbles, which helps with cleaning.

Micelle

DIRT

Head end is hydrophilic

Tail end is hydrophobic

Surfactant molecule

Dirt is trapped in the center

HOW DO SURFACTANTS WORK?

Surfactant molecules have one end that is hydrophilic (attracted to water) and one that is hydrophobic (repelled by water). The hydrophobic ends are attracted to dirty, greasy particles that cannot dissolve in water. They cluster around dirt, so that the hydrophilic parts of the molecules point into the water. This makes a ball-shaped micelle, which hides away dirt and is easily washed away by water.

THE CHEMISTRY OF BREAD

The secret to light, springy bread is in chemistry. What turns a sticky, doughy lump into a soft, risen loaf of bread is a chemical reaction that produces gas inside the dough as it cooks, helped by the heat of the oven. The gas bubbles grow in size while the bread bakes, making the bread light and aerated.

KNEADING

An important step in making bread is kneading. The dough is pummeled and pulled, which makes proteins from the flour combine, creating long, stretchy strands of gluten. This gluten makes the dough elastic. The stretchy elastic dough traps air bubbles in the bread as it bakes, so the finished loaf is full of small, light holes. Traditionally, bread was kneaded by hand, and many bakers and people still make bread in this way.

YEAST

Making bread that rises into a bigger, fluffy loaf requires a raising agent, such as yeast. Yeast is a tiny microorganism. When it is mixed with warm water and the sugars naturally found in flour, the yeast springs into action. Its molecules "eat" the sugar molecules and produce bubbles of carbon dioxide.

Carbon dioxide

Sugar molecule

Yeast molecule

THE CHORLEYWOOD PROCESS

In the 1960s, chemical engineers in Britain came up with a new way of making bread—the Chorleywood process. This method produces bread that is softer, lasts twice as long, and is much cheaper and quicker to make than handmade bread. Each slice in a Chorleywood loaf is identical, so shoppers know exactly what they are getting each time. Here are some features of the Chorleywood process:

Bread improver
A chemical bread "improver" is added to the dough. These chemicals allow the bread to be made more quickly and cheaply than is possible using a traditional method.

Fast-rising dough
The enzymes in the improver also make the yeast work harder and help the dough expand, while oxidizing agents trap gas from the yeast. This means the bread does not need to be left to "rise."

High speed mixing
Machines mix up large batches of dough in just five minutes—kneading by hand is a slow process by comparison. Enzymes in the improver make the dough strong and easy to mix.

Long-life bread
Fats in the improver allow Chorleywood bread to last for a long time without going stale or moldy. Handmade bread generally needs to be eaten the same day it is baked.

Downsides
Most of the bread in Britain is now made using this process. However, there is a downside: Chorleywood bread contains chemical additives and is lower in nutrients than traditional bread.

DRINKING WATER

Nobody can live without clean water. We need it for washing, cooking, and flushing toilets. But most of all we need it to drink, and for that it has to be absolutely safe. Water companies work hard to make sure that our drinking water is safe, which involves a lot of chemical tests. Water is pumped into water treatment plants from reservoirs, aquifers (underground stores of water), and streams. This water contains a mixture of bacteria, viruses, and other chemical pollutants that need to be removed at the water treatment plant. Machines test how acidic and dirty the water is as it enters the plant so that the treatment can be tweaked to match each batch of water. The water is then treated in a number of different ways, making it safe for us to drink.

The coagulant is released into the water.

Mixer paddle

1. SCREENING

First, the water is screened to remove large solids such as twigs and leaves.

2. COAGULATION

Next, coagulants (chemicals such as aluminum sulfate) are stirred into the water to remove sediment and undissolved particles. These coagulants attract particles so that they clump together into bigger pieces, which are called **floc**.

3. CLARIFICATION

Then the floc is removed from the water. This can be done by leaving the floc to sink to the bottom of the water tank, with the cleaner water slowly flowing off from the top, into a second tank. Another way is to pump air into the water, so that air bubbles stick to the floc and make the particles float to the top, where they form a "sludge blanket." The sludge blanket is scooped off, while the cleaner water underneath flows off into the next tank.

4. FILTRATION

To remove the last tiny solid particle, the water is pushed through layers of carbon, sand, and gravel filters so that it at least looks clean.

The water toward the top of the tank is cleaner, as the floc sinks to the bottom.

Flow of cleaner water

Particle of floc

Layer of sludge

Coal (carbon)

Sand

Gravel

CHLORINE

Chlorine is a chemical that is often used to treat drinking water. The world safety standard for drinking water is one part of chlorine per million parts of water. Water in swimming pools contains three times this amount—it won't harm you to swim in it, but you shouldn't guzzle down a glass of pool water! Chlorine in drinking water is perfectly safe to drink, though some people don't like the taste.

5. DISINFECTION

Finally, the water is treated with chemicals to remove any microorganisms that could be dangerous. Chlorine and ozone are pumped through the water. They kill off any viruses, germs, and fungi.

Chemically-treated water

Clean drinking water

SODAS

Have you noticed how sodas aren't actually fizzy until you open them for the first time? Trapped inside the drink is the chemistry that is needed to make the drink fizzy, which is only activated when the can or bottle is first opened.

HOW IS FIZZY SODA MADE?

The fizz comes from bubbles of carbon dioxide escaping from the drink. Carbon dioxide is a gas. To capture it in a drink, the gas must be made to dissolve into liquid. In order for water molecules to trap carbon dioxide, the process must be undertaken at **low temperature** and under **high pressure**.

Carbon dioxide + water = carbonic acid

This chemical reaction is reversible—carbonic acid can easily return to being just carbon dioxide and water. To keep the carbon dioxide dissolved as carbonic acid, cans and bottles are sealed so they are airtight, which keeps the pressure inside constant. The moment you open a drink, the carbon dioxide begins to escape from the liquid .

Carbonated (fizzy) water

Carbon dioxide

WHY DO DRINKS GO FLAT?

Because only a certain amount of carbon dioxide is dissolved in a drink, eventually it will all escape. Once the fizzy bubbles have gone, the drink becomes flat. This happens more quickly in warmer temperatures.

WHY DOES STILL WATER GO BUBBLY?

You might notice bubbles forming in a glass of water that is left alone for a while. This is because other gases from the air are naturally dissolved in water. If the water starts off cold and gradually warms up to room temperature, bubbles of carbon dioxide and other gases will slowly escape the liquid and form bubbles.

BATH FIZZERS

When you drop a bath fizzer into your nice warm bath, it bubbles into a colorful, fragrant explosion. But why? It's all about chemistry. Read on to learn how a few simple ingredients can fill your bath with fun.

DID YOU KNOW?

Bath fizzers contain baking soda, citric acid, cornstarch, fragrance, and color. See pages 42 and 43 to learn how to combine these ingredients and make one for yourself.

CHEMICAL REACTION

The fizz is the reaction of the baking soda and citric acid when they meet the water of the bath. They both dissolve very easily into the water, and as they mix together in the water they create another chemical reaction, which causes the fizzer to froth.

The carbonate part of the baking soda meets with the hydrogen part of the citric acid, and together they create carbon dioxide. This gas escapes from the water, creating fizzy bubbles.

Because bath fizzers are spherical, they keep fizzing for a while as the outer edges react with the water and dissolve. Gradually the bomb gets smaller as the water eats it away from the outside in. This is where the cornstarch is important: it slows the reaction down by slowing down the rate at which the baking soda and citric acid can dissolve in the water. Without it, the bath bomb would fizz out in seconds rather than minutes.

ON THE FARM

Over the past fifty years, the world's farms have more than doubled the amount of food they produce. This is partly thanks to chemicals, which have helped crops grow reliably and kept farm animals healthy so they can produce more meat and milk. By 2050 we will have to produce half again as much food, to feed a world population of almost 10 billion people! Chemicals have helped us so far, but they have also created some problems. Understanding the chemistry and biology of the land and what we put into it helps us save the planet while also keeping everybody fed.

PESTICIDES—PROS

We plant crops for us to harvest and eat, but we aren't the only living things that like to eat them. "Pests" such as caterpillars, beetles, and aphids often get there first. The more they eat, the less there is for us. Pesticides are chemicals that are sprayed onto crops to kill off these insects and keep the crops safe. Whole fields can be sprayed with pesticides by a spinning crop sprayer or by an airplane.

FERTILIZERS—PROS

As crops grow, they take nutrients from the land. Growing the same crops on the same land year after year leaves the land starved of good nutrients. Fertilizers are chemicals that put nutrients back into the land to help the plants grow.

WHAT'S THE ALTERNATIVE?

Organic farming is a farming approach that does not use any synthetic chemicals. There are also other chemical-free ways to deal with weeds, pests, and nutrients. Here are a few examples:

Genetic modification is a laboratory technique. It can create plants that are resistant to drought or pests, or that are able to grow in tough conditions.

Underground farming uses LED lights to give plants the energy they need to grow. Because the space is enclosed, the environment can be controlled, and pesticides aren't needed because pests can't get in in the first place.

Crop rotation is a technique that has been used for hundreds of years. Different crops are planted in turn on the same piece of land. Each crop takes slightly different nutrients from the soil, helping the soil recover more easily.

Biological control uses other creatures to control pests—for example, ladybugs, which love to eat aphids.

PESTICIDES—CONS

Pesticides are harmful to all insects, not just the ones that eat our crops. Some insects do important jobs, such as pollinating plants so that they can grow again the next year. All insects are at least a delicious meal for another animal, such as small birds. If we kill off insects, we reduce the biodiversity of the whole area.

FERTILIZERS—CONS

Often more fertilizer is put onto land than can be used by the crops. When it rains, the chemicals run off the fields and into waterways. If they gather in ponds and lakes, they can "fertilize" the water, making it easy for pond weeds and algae to grow. Algae can grow so that it covers the whole surface of the water. This means light can't get through and any plants and fish below the surface will die.

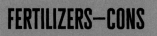

SEEING OUR INSIDES

Biomedical engineering has made it possible for doctors to see inside our bodies without needing to cut us open. This helps doctors figure out what might be going on inside us when we complain about feeling unwell.

X-RAYS

The first technique for seeing beneath our skin came in 1895. Wilhelm Röntgen had been experimenting with cathode rays, which are glass tubes containing gas and an electrical current. He aimed the rays at a chemically treated screen, and when he placed his hand in the way of the rays, he found it made an image of his bones on the screen. X-rays are used to take still images of a particular part of the body.

DID YOU KNOW?

X-rays were given their name because the scientist who discovered them didn't know what they were! In the 1950s, they were used to check the fit of people's shoes. This stopped when scientists realized how dangerous X-rays could be. Hospitals make sure that taking X-rays is as safe as possible for the patient.

ULTRASOUND

Sound waves travel from the ultrasound scanner into the part of the body the doctor wants to look at. Different tissues "echo" the waves back to the scanner differently, and the computer translates those echoes into images on a screen. Ultrasound waves are not dangerous, so they can be used to look at babies growing inside their mothers.

MRI SCANS

MRI stands for Magnetic Resonance Imaging. It uses magnetic fields and radio waves to interact with tiny positive charges inside each atom, called protons, giving a picture of our insides. Magnets and radio waves are safe to use inside the body, but MRI scanners are expensive to use, and the patient needs to lie very still inside the large, noisy machine.

BIOMATERIALS

A biomaterial is something that has been made to help with a medical problem. It could be added to the body to improve the way it works, to help repair any broken parts, or to monitor something inside the body. People have been using biomaterials for hundreds of years, but they have become ever more sophisticated. More exciting developments will come during your lifetime!

STITCHES

The stitches used to sew up a wound are called sutures. Sewing a wound closed helps it heal by bringing the "raw" edges together and keeping them closed, so dirt and germs can't get in while the layers of skin knit back together. Sutures have been used since ancient times, with catgut or silk as the thread. They were even used in ancient Rome.

BLISTER CUSHIONS

Hydrocolloid bandages contain a substance that absorbs water. They are used to help heal blisters. The bandage covers the blister, protecting it and cushioning the area, while also absorbing liquid from the blister. Each bandage can absorb 28 times its own weight in water! The closed, moist environment around the blister helps it heal.

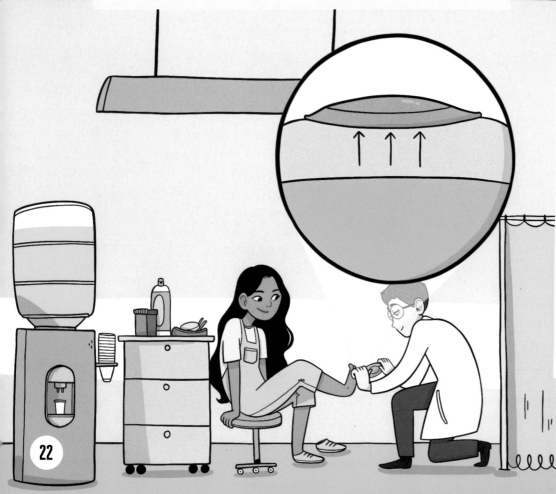

SKIN ADHESIVE

Instead of stitching wounds shut with sutures, special glue can be used. It holds the edges of the wound in place while protecting the wound. On deep cuts, stitches might be used for the deeper layers while the "glue" is used on the top layer, to help keep the deep stitches in place.

ELECTRONIC TATTOOS

These devices can be stuck onto the skin to measure things such as heart rate, brain waves, and muscle activity. Their thin wires are arranged in wave patterns inside sticky material so that the tattoo can squeeze and stretch as the person moves. Electronic tattoos can last for up to 24 hours. In the future they could be used to monitor newborn babies, to help wounds heal, or to treat burns.

DELIVERING MEDICINE

Biomedical engineers also think of ways to deliver medicine to the right part of the body. Stomach acid is so powerful that it can attack medicines. Some medicines can also irritate the stomach—such as ibuprofen, which can cause stomach ulcers. Drug designers coat pills with a polymer that is resistant to stomach acid so that the medicine is only released into the body in the intestine, where it is quickly absorbed.

MALARIA

Malaria is a disease that kills more than 600,000 people each year. It occurs in places where the mosquitoes are infected with a malaria parasite. When one of these mosquitoes bites you, some of the parasite enters your blood and travels around your body. The first symptoms are a headache, fever, and chills, which are so common that people might not realize at first that they have the disease. If it isn't treated, malaria can quickly get much worse and even cause death. Biomedical engineering has come up with different ways to protect people from the disease.

Mosquito nets

The holes in these thin nylon nets are too small for mosquitoes to fly through, so they are a simple way to stop mosquitoes from reaching you. They are particularly useful over a bed, so people can sleep safely at night. Mosquito nets are cheap and easy to distribute, but they only work if they're used properly: any rips must be repaired, and the net must be completely sealed and tucked under the bed.

Quinine

Quinine has been used against malaria in Europe for almost 400 years. It is made from the bark of the cinchona tree. Quinine works because as it flows through the blood it stops the malaria parasite from thriving. Quinine does cure some forms of malaria, but it can come with side effects, such as headache, nausea, and hearing loss, so other, laboratory-made medicines can be better options.

Repellant sprays

Mosquito repellents are chemical barriers that make mosquitoes not want to bite you. It is female mosquitoes that bite us—they need protein from our blood to help them make eggs. They "smell" our skin and are attracted to the carbon dioxide we give off. Sprays work by masking the smell of skin, but they wear off over time so need to be reapplied to keep working.

TU YOUYOU (BORN 1930)

Tu Youyou combined her western medical training with traditional Chinese medical knowledge to create a medicine that has saved millions of lives.

Youyou was born in China in 1930. At sixteen she had tuberculosis, which kept her out of school for two years. When she returned she knew she wanted to become a medical researcher.

Youyou studied pharmacy at Beijing Medical College, where she learned how to extract active ingredients from plants and figure out the chemical structures of those ingredients. Later, she studied traditional Chinese medicine.

In 1967, Chairman Mao, the leader of China, launched a project to find a new cure for malaria. In 1969, Youyou became head of the project. She had to leave her children for three years so she could concentrate on her work.

Youyou consulted ancient medical texts and found thousands of recipes against malaria. One recipe mentioned steeping the herb sweet wormwood in cold water. Youyou realized her usual method for extracting the medicine, which involved boiling water, might have killed off the active ingredient.

Her personal sacrifice paid off: in 1972 she produced a nontoxic medicine that cured malaria in monkeys. Youyou and her team took the medicine themselves to test it—and found it was safe.

CHINESE MEDICINE WILL HELP US CONQUER LIFE-THREATENING DISEASES WORLDWIDE, AND PEOPLE ACROSS THE GLOBE WILL ENJOY ITS BENEFITS.

In 2015, Youyou was awarded the Nobel Prize in Physiology or Medicine for her work.

RUNNING BLADES

Running blades are prosthetic lower limbs for people who have had leg amputations. They are different from prosthetic legs for walking on: blades are designed for running. Their curved shape and strong, flexible carbon fiber mean runners can go much faster than they could using traditional prosthetics that replicate the look of human bones.

INSPIRATION

The first running blade was designed in the 1970s by American inventor Van Philips. He was an amputee himself, and he named it the "Flex-Foot." Van Philips was inspired by fast-traveling animals such as cheetahs and kangaroos, and by the way diving boards and pole vaulting can propel people a long way. He realized that it's not the bone structure of human legs that gives power, but the tendons and ligaments.

IMPROVEMENTS

The Cheetah blade, launched for athletes in 1996, mimics the backward curve of a cheetah's leg. When the runner steps down onto it, the blade stores up kinetic energy, which then releases as it pushes the runner forward.

MARKUS REHM (BORN 1988)

Markus Rehm is a German Paralympic athlete who won the long jump world title in 2011 and has been smashing his own records ever since. Rehm was born in Göppingen, Germany, in 1988. When he was fourteen years old, he had an accident while wakeboarding, and his right leg was amputated below the knee. Rehm was training to be a prosthetist (someone who fits prosthetics) when he started doing athletics. When a coach gave him his first running blade, he knew what an expensive gift it was and realized that the coach was investing in him as an athlete. Rehm first beat the long jump world record in 2011, jumping 7.09 m. He broke the world record again in 2012 (7.35 m), 2015 (8.40 m), 2018 (8.48 m), and 2021 (8.62 m). Markus has won three Paralympic gold medals and one bronze.

THERE'S NO "I CAN'T"

MODERN RUNNING BLADES

Today running blades are made from around 80 very thin layers of carbon fiber. The more layers, the stronger the blade. Running blades are tailored to the wearer, as different people have different length legs, had their legs amputated in different places—above or below the knee—and could have one or two amputations. Running blades are also shaped differently for sprinters, who need short bursts of energy, than for those who run greater distances over longer times.

TISSUE ENGINEERING

Tissue engineers use biological and synthetic materials to create living tissue in a laboratory. The aim is to transplant the engineered tissue into a living body. This new tissue would work like normal tissue and can be made to replace damaged or diseased tissue that doesn't work properly.

WHAT IS TISSUE?

Tissue is a collection of cells that work together to do a particular job. Several different types of tissues might work together in a single organ, such as a heart.

FOUR FACTORS

Tissue engineering needs four main things:

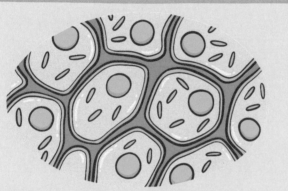

Cells These need to be the right cells to do the job. If skin tissue is being engineered, skin cells are needed. Cells are taken directly from a patient or grown in a lab from the patient's stem cells. Stem cells are cells that are not specialized to do any particular job but that can be made to grow into specialized cells.

Environment This is the place where the cells will grow. It is often a "scaffold" made from synthetic material and shaped like the final piece of tissue— if new ear tissue is being made, it could be shaped like an ear. Once the cells have grown, the scaffold might dissolve, or stay to shape the tissue.

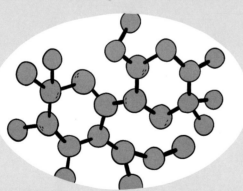

Biomolecules These are the chemicals that the cells need to grow and reproduce so that they can develop in their environment. They are the same chemicals that would be found inside a living body.

Physical force The cells need to be encouraged to develop and grow into tissue. This is done by pushing, pulling, or moving the cells around in their environment.

A COMPLEX FUTURE

There is still a lot to be figured out in the world of tissue engineering. Tissues such as bladders, small arteries, skin grafts, and cartilage have already been successfully created and transplanted. Engineers are working toward being able to make more complex combinations of tissues that work together.

WEIRD SCIENCE

Growing a human ear on the back of a mouse might sound and look weird, but this was one of the first major breakthroughs in tissue engineering. The work didn't do much for the mouse, but it did help scientists develop the skills to grow a new ear for children born with defective or missing ears, using the children's own cells.

1. The patients had their "good" ear scanned.

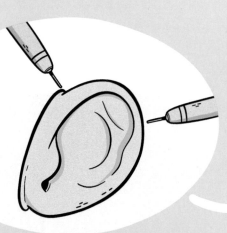

2. A scaffold was 3D-printed to match the scan of the good ear. Cells taken from the defective ear were seeded onto the scaffold and then left to grow for three months.

3. The newly grown ears were then grafted on to the patients. In the future, we might be able to grow whole organs to replace damaged or diseased organs, using a patient's own cells.

GETTING OLDER

People born today can expect to live to more than 70 years of age. A hundred years ago, life expectancy was much lower. One reason we are living longer is that we have found medicines to cure many of the diseases that used to kill people. Long life doesn't always mean being fit and active though—the longer you live, the more likely you are to develop an age-related condition, such as diabetes or dementia. As people grow old they want to continue to live independent lives for as long as possible. There are a numer of biomedical tools that can help.

FINDING DISEASES EARLY

The earlier doctors can spot a disease developing, the more they can do to help. The eye disease glaucoma is most common in people in their 70s and 80s, and if it's left untreated, people can lose their sight. Eye doctors can spot the early signs of glaucoma from scans, and the earlier it's spotted, the better it can be treated. Artificial intelligence (AI) can help eye doctors by sorting through scans just as accurately as a human, but much more quickly.

KEEPING SAFE

Biomedical engineers have developed all kinds of wearable technology to help keep patients living independently, without needing to be in the hospital or regularly visited by health workers. Monitoring devices can be worn close to the skin or even inside the body. They allow patients to go about their daily lives, safe in the knowledge that a doctor or family members will be alerted if something goes wrong.

HEART MONITOR

Machines that record a person's heart beats used to be available only at hospitals or doctor's offices. Now, portable devices can show how the heart works in real time, while allowing a patient to continue normal life. Small heart-monitoring devices can connect to a smart phone. The user places two fingers from each hand on two sensors for 30 seconds, which allows an app to detect if their heart rhythm is normal. For people without a known heart issue, smart watches can monitor heart health and let them know if anything seems unusual.

FIGHTING LONELINESS

Living independently in old age can be lonely. More than a quarter of Japan's population is over age 65. To help care for the elderly, the government is employing robots! Paro is a therapeutic robot seal that is soft and acts like a real animal—it can be active or sleepy, and it responds to facial expressions and being petted. Because it is so cute and responds to its owner, it can help the elderly feel an emotional connection in the times between visits from caregivers, friends, and family.

FEEDING THE WORLD

Farming animals for meat takes up a lot of land, and there's not enough land on on the planet to feed the whole world population meat every day. However, it's not just space that's a problem. Farming animals takes up a lot of resources (particularly water) and reduces biodiversity, which we need for a healthy planet.

Coming to the rescue are chemical engineers. They are developing ways to produce meat and dairy products, or things that taste just like them, with the same nutrients and far less environmental impact. These foods aren't farmed, but grown in laboratories.

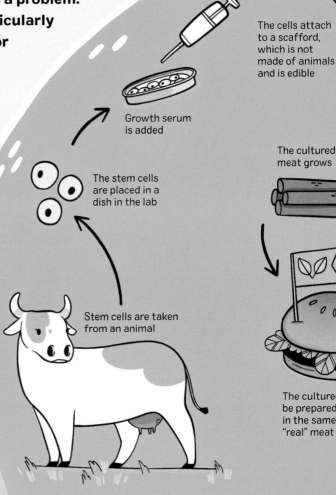

Growth serum is added

The cells attach to a scafford, which is not made of animals and is edible

The stem cells are placed in a dish in the lab

The cultured meat grows

Stem cells are taken from an animal

The cultured meat can be prepared and eaten in the same way as "real" meat

PLANT-BASED MEAT

For decades we have been using vegetarian products such as tofu, jackfruit, and soy protein to make food that looks and behaves in a similar way to meat. Like meat, these foods are high in protein and calcium. To some, however, they don't taste meaty enough. Now, one company has found the molecule that makes meat taste meaty. It is called heme, and it can be made (or "brewed") in a laboratory, then added to plant-based meat substitutes.

CELL-CULTURED MEAT

Cell-cultured meat is identical to meat that comes from farm-raised animals but is made in a laboratory. It uses 99% less land and 96% less water than farming animals, and causes no harm to the animals. Cell-cultured meat uses the same technology as tissue engineering. Stem cells are taken from the animals and cultured in big stainless steel tanks in laboratories. They are given nutrients and growth factors to make the muscle tissue grow.

A new gene is inserted into a bacterial plasmid (small circle of DNA)

A section of the gene is cut out

The engineered bacteria are grown in a culture, to produce more of them

The bacterium now contains engineered plasmids

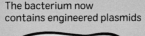

The bacteria produce milk protein, which is then added to water, creating a drink identical to milk

BREWED MILK

The dairy industry produces 4% of our greenhouse gas emissions—more than the shipping and aviation industries combined! Making dairy products without keeping dairy animals would be much better for the environment. Chemical engineers have developed "precision fermentation"—a way of using microorganisms to produce milk. "Brewing" milk in this way allows us to make dairy products without farm animals. Milk is a mixture of six different proteins, fat, sugar, and minerals, all mixed in water. These ingredients can be precision brewed and mixed into water to make milk that tastes just like the milk we know.

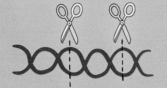

GENETIC ENGINEERING

Genetic engineering is key to many of these new processes. It involves looking through the DNA of the animal or plant you want to copy and finding the gene for making the protein you want. That gene is then cloned (which means making more copies of it) and inserted into the DNA of a microorganism such as a bacterium, yeast, or fungus. Then the microorganism can get on with its life, which now involves producing the protein we want.

OTHER NONANIMAL PRODUCTS

The same principles can be used to make other products we have taken from animals, such as silk, fur, wool, horn, and leather.

PANDEMICS

The Covid-19 pandemic has highlighted how important biomedical innovation is in keeping us all healthy. When the pandemic was first announced, we didn't know how the virus spread between people, or how to treat people who were suffering and dying from the disease. Health-care workers and biomedical scientists from around the world worked together and shared their information and insights, allowing us to fight the virus.

Early in the pandemic, scientists knew that the virus was **transmitted** through the air. People were urged to keep away from each other, to use hand sanitizer, and to wash their groceries. Then the virus was found to be spreading between people who hadn't been close together—the virus could survive in droplets in the air. Scientists studied these patterns of transmission to learn which activities were the most risky.

Testing for Covid-19 usually involves a swab test, where the nose or back of the throat are wiped with a cotton swab. This is not new technology, and neither are the rapid lateral flow tests used to test the swabs at home. What is new is that people have been able to access these tests fairly easily and keep infection from spreading.

Scientists **monitor** where Covid-19 numbers are growing and how the virus is changing. In many countries people report their symptoms and test results, so scientists can see where the virus is most common. Some countries look at the genetic sequences of the samples that come into their labs so that they can see where new variants of the virus have developed.

Vaccines work by introducing a small amount of the disease to the body so that the immune system can learn to fight it. They are usually given as injections. The mRNA vaccine was used for the first time in the Covid-19 pandemic. Its success has led scientists to try this technology out against other diseases.

KATALIN KARIKÓ
(BORN 1955)

Katalin Karikó is a Hungarian-American biochemist who pioneered the new mRNA vaccine. It was used during the Covid-19 pandemic and was so successful that it is already being developed for many more lifesaving vaccinations.

Karikó grew up in Hungary in a small house without running water, a refrigerator, or television. She loved science and earned a PhD in biochemistry. Karikó left Hungary for the United States in 1985. She traveled with her husband, her two-year-old daughter, a teddy bear stuffed with money, and an idea for curing diseases.

Karikó's idea was to find a way to get the body to make its own cure to fight the diseases invading it. Years after she had this idea, the first mRNA vaccine became one of the more effective vaccines against Covid-19.

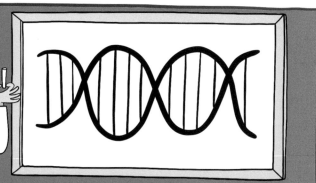

What is mRNA?
Your cells are filled with DNA, a library of information. mRNA is a molecule that copies a small part of your DNA and takes it to the ribosomes (protein factories inside the cell). The ribosomes read the DNA instructions and use them to create a protein.

Karikó and her team worked hard over many years to find a way to safely give the body new mRNA that contained the instructions to make small pieces of a virus, so that the body could make antibodies against it.

When the Covid-19 pandemic hit, Karikó was working on using mRNA to fight cancer—without any luck so far. She switched her work to making a vaccine against Covid-19. It was produced at record speed.

The success of the mRNA vaccines against Covid-19 has encouraged researchers all over the world to try out the technology against other diseases. mRNA vaccines are safer than traditional vaccines and can be manufactured much more quickly.

WHAT'S NEXT?

Biomedical engineers are busy working on all kinds of amazing technological innovations that will be part of the future and could be everyday news within your lifetime. Here are just a few of them.

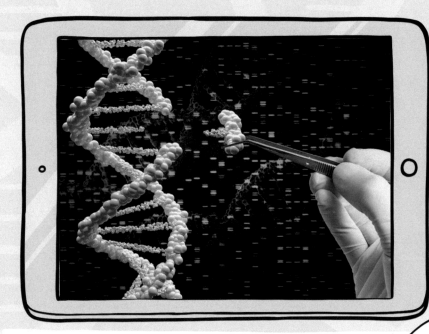

GENE EDITING

Gene editing involves taking out a gene—a part of the chromosome—that might be faulty and replacing it with one that is not faulty or that does a better job. Editing genes has been possible for a while—for example, genetically modified (GM) crops are designed to withstand difficulties such as disease and drought. CRISPR is a new tool for gene editing that is more convenient and less time-consuming than older methods. It has already been used to create a tomato that contains high concentrations of a chemical that aids relaxation.

JENNIFER DOUDNA
(BORN 1964)

THE MORE WE KNOW, THE MORE WE REALIZE THERE IS TO KNOW!

Dr. Jennifer Doudna is one of the scientists who developed the CRISPR technology for editing genes. She grew up in Hawaii and earned a PhD from Harvard Medical School. In 2012 Doudna and her collaborator Emmanuelle Charpentier suggested that a tool that certain bacteria have to protect themselves against viruses could be used to edit the genomes of other organisms. Eight years later, she and Charpentier received the Nobel Prize in Chemistry for their idea. The CRISPR tool is a protein (a large biological molecule) that works like scissors to cut up the DNA of invading viruses so that it isn't able to infect the bacteria. Doudna and Charpentier figured out how to program the protein to cut up and edit DNA in other organisms.

XENOTRANSPLANTATION

One way of helping a patient with a diseased organ, such as their liver or heart, is by taking it out and transplanting a healthy organ in its place. The main problem with organ transplants is that there aren't enough good organs available. One option could be xenotransplantation: transplanting a healthy organ from another species. However, other animals have viruses that the human immune system would not recognize and would attack. CRISPR gene editing can remove the genes that would trigger this immune response. Xenotransplantation is still in its very early stages, but 2022 saw the first successful transplant of a pig heart into a human.

BIONANOTECHNOLOGY

Bionanomaterials are the molecules that are the building blocks of all life—things such as DNA, proteins, sugars, and fats. Scientists research bionanomaterials to find tools that are useful precisely because they are so small: they can move inside the body and target very specific areas—for example, by delivering medicine only to the part of the body that needs it. This could be done by attaching medicine to nanomagnetic particles, then using a magnetic field to attract the medicine to the right place. Precision targeting is more effective than when you take regular medicine, which travels all around the body and can produce unwanted side effects.

RECYCLING

Chemical engineers are working on different ways to recycle and make better use of waste products. Some materials, such as aluminum, can easily be recycled and used again, while others, particularly plastics, are much harder. Throwing away waste products pollutes land and sea, and if small animals eat them by accident, the toxins can build up in the food chain, which could poison us all.

ALUMINUM

Aluminum cans are one of the easiest things to recycle. About two-thirds of all the aluminum products that have ever been made are still in use. Pure aluminum is very stable—it can be melted down and reused many times without losing quality. Here's how aluminum is recycled:

1. The recycled cans are sorted to remove pieces of trash and anything made of iron or other metals such as brass, copper, and zinc.

2. The aluminum cans are crushed into square bales.

3. The bales are melted down into new sheets of aluminum.

To recycle a can takes about 5% of the energy needed to make a can out of new materials.

4. Used cans can be recycled and back in stores within three months!

PLASTICS

Plastics can be recycled in a few different ways. Reusing plastic such as a takeout food container is better than throwing it in the recycling. Plastic bottles can't be reused for a new customer because they aren't clean or strong enough, so they should be reused for as long as possible before being recycled.

When you do throw plastic into the recycling, the bottles are melted down and remolded, but in the process the plastic loses its strength and flexibility. This means it can't be used again as bottles, but only as something with lower value. Plastic can't be "downcycled" like this forever; eventually the plastic is no longer useful and new plastic is needed to make new items.

Plastics are made up of long strings of molecules called "polymers." When plastic is broken down into its monomer building blocks, it can be remade again as "new." However, this takes a huge amount of energy—plastic only melts at 600–900°F (300–500°C). Chemical engineering could be a cheaper way to get plastic back to its starting blocks. Chemically recycled plastic could possibly be reused over and over again, like aluminum.

JAMIE GARCIA
(BORN 1983)

Jamie Garcia is a scientist at IBM who researches ways to chemically recycle plastics. This could help get rid of plastic waste and reduce our need to dig up oil to create new plastic. She found a catalyst (a chemical that speeds up a chemical reaction without being used up itself) that breaks down the plastic from used CDs so that it can be remade into something else. It created polysulfone, which is used to purify water. Garcia also realized that energy could be saved by designing plastics with a built-in ability to self-destruct when they were no longer useful. She found a strong plastic that could be broken down in acid and then reused.

39

ACID TEST

Chemists measure how acidic or alkaline a substance is using the pH scale. You can create your own pH solution using a red cabbage. Then test it out in your kitchen!

YOU WILL NEED
- Red cabbage (about one-fourth)
- A sieve or strainer
- Water
- Vinegar
- Carbonated water
- An egg
- Three clear glasses
- A pitcher

INSTRUCTIONS

1. First we need to extract the purple color from the cabbage. Chop or tear up the cabbage leaves and soak them in hot water. Then wait for the water to cool.

2. Pour the cabbage mixture through a sieve or strainer and collect the purple water in a pitcher. You can now discard the cabbage pieces.

3. Pour a little of the purple water into the three glasses—they should be no more than half full.

4. Slowly pour some vinegar into the first cup. If no changes happen, add a little more. What do you see?

5. Into the second cup, pour in carbonated water. Does this make a different change or the same one?

6. Add some beaten egg into the third cup. What happens here?

WHAT'S THE SCIENCE?
The cabbage turns the water purple because purple chemicals dissolve in the water. The cabbage water is called an "indicator" solution, because it changes color when acid or alkali solutions are added to it. When different liquids mix with the cabbage water, chemical reactions take place, which cause the color changes.

HOW SOAP WORKS

Water is not very good at cleaning things by itself because it has such strong surface tension (see pages 10 and 11). This experiment shows how soap can help clean things by breaking down the water's surface tension.

YOUR TURN!

YOU WILL NEED
- A bowl of water
- Ground black pepper
- A toothpick
- Dishwashing liquid

INSTRUCTIONS

1. Sprinkle some ground black pepper over the top of the bowl of water. It should float on the water's surface.

2. Touch the end of the toothpick into the dishwashing liquid so that its point is coated with a little soap.

3. Touch the soapy end of the toothpick to the surface of the water, then watch what happens to the black pepper.

WHAT'S THE SCIENCE?

The soap breaks down the water's surface tension. The pepper shoots across the water away from the soap in the places where the surface tension is still intact. Eventually, with enough soap, the pepper will start falling to the bottom of the bowl.

TAKE IT FURTHER

Try this experiment with other small, light objects that can balance on the surface of water. What can you find? You could try a single unused staple, glitter, or pencil shavings.

CHEMISTRY IN THE BATH

Bath fizzers use chemistry to make bath time fun! Plus they are easy to make.

YOUR TURN!

YOU WILL NEED

- 3.5 oz. (100 g) baking soda
- 1.75 oz. (50 g) citric acid
- 1 oz. (25 g) cornstarch
- 2 tbsp. oil (sunflower, coconut, or olive oil are all good)
- ¼ tsp. or a few drops of essential oil to make it smell nice (lavender is good for relaxing)
- A few drops of food coloring
- A medium or large mixing bowl
- A whisk
- A small mixing bowl
- Molds—silicone cupcake cases work well, or small yogurt containers or even cookie cutter shapes

INSTRUCTIONS

1. Mix the baking soda, citric acid, and cornstarch in the bowl, whisking gently to combine.

2. In the small mixing bowl, combine the oil, essential oil, and food coloring. Don't worry if the food coloring doesn't dissolve into the oils—it will all mix nicely in the powders.

3. Add a teaspoon of the oils to the powders and use the whisk to combine. As you bash the whisk around the bowl, the coloring droplets will dye the powders.

1

2

3

42

4. Repeat, whisking after each addition of liquid, until all the oil is mixed into the powder.

5. You might want to add a few drops of water now to help the mixture combine. Make sure you only add a few drops—any more and the mixture might start fizzing! It should look like damp sand and clump together when you squeeze it.

6. Pack the mixture tightly into the molds. Press it down and smooth the top with the back of a teaspoon.

7. Leave to dry for 2 to 4 hours, and then carefully remove the molds. The bath fizzers are ready to use!

LEMONADE FIZZ

Carbonated drinks fizz because of carbon dioxide gas escaping from the liquid (see page 16). This experiment shows you how to make a carbonated homemade lemonade!

(see page 16)

YOUR TURN!

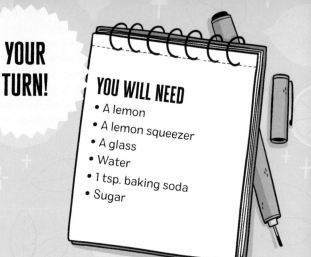

YOU WILL NEED
- A lemon
- A lemon squeezer
- A glass
- Water
- 1 tsp. baking soda
- Sugar

INSTRUCTIONS

1. Squeeze the juice from the lemon into a large glass.

2. Add an equal volume of water to the lemon juice.

3. Taste, and add some sugar to make it sweeter.

4. Stir in the baking soda, then drink!

WHAT'S THE SCIENCE?
Lemon juice contains citric acid. When the baking soda reacts with the citric acid, it creates carbon dioxide, which leaves the liquid as bubbles—just like you see when you open a soda can. This is the same reaction that happens when you put a bath fizzer into water.

BOUNCY EGG

Raw eggs are fragile, and their shells can easily smash if they are dropped. Between the crunchy shell and the liquid egg part is a thick membrane. By dissolving the shell, the raw egg can be turned into a bouncy ball!

YOUR TURN!

YOU WILL NEED
- An egg
- A clear glass
- White vinegar

INSTRUCTIONS

1. Carefully put the raw egg into the glass.

2. Pour white vinegar into the glass until the egg is covered.

3. Now leave the egg for two days. You might see little gas bubbles forming on the outside of the shell.

4. After two days, check the egg—its shell should have disintegrated. Take it out of the vinegar. You might need to gently rub the surface to get rid of any last pieces of shell.

5. The egg is now (a little) bouncy! But be careful—the membrane is not super-strong and will still break if "bounced" too hard, leaving an eggy mess to clear up!

WHAT'S THE SCIENCE?
Egg shell is made from calcium carbonate, which dissolves in acid, such as vinegar. The membrane doesn't dissolve in vinegar so is left, holding the egg intact. The gas bubbles on the outside of the shell are carbon dioxide, which results from the chemical reaction.

TAKE IT FURTHER
You could give your bouncy egg color! Before starting, squeeze the color from a highlighter (take out the cylinder and squeeze the ink) into the jar. Then add your egg and vinegar as usual.

45

GLOSSARY

Aluminum
A metal that is used to make foil and beverage cans, which can easily be recycled.

Bionanotechnology
Engineering with tiny biological building blocks.

Carbon dioxide
A greenhouse gas that helps keep the planet warm. It's produced by all animals and by burning fossil fuels. Too much carbon dioxide is contributing to global warming and climate change.

Chlorine
A chemical that helps disinfect water.

Cohesion
A force that keeps molecules in a liquid together.

CRISPR
A technology for quickly and easily editing genes.

Disinfectant
Chemicals that make surfaces safe by killing microorganisms that could cause diseases, such as bacteria and molds.

Fertilizer
Chemicals used on land to help encourage crops to grow.

Fossil fuel
A fuel such as coal, oil, or natural gas that is extracted from the ground and burned to produce electricity. Burning fossil fuels creates greenhouse gases.

Genetic engineering
Using chemicals to change part of a cell's genetic code, or DNA.

Gluten
Long, stretchy strands of proteins made from kneading flour to make bread.

Greenhouse gas
A gas such as carbon dioxide or methane that helps keep the planet warm. Greenhouses gases cause global warming and climate change.

Heme
A natural chemical that makes meat taste meaty.

Hydrophilic
A chemical that is attracted to water.

Hydrophobic
A chemical that is repelled by water.

Micelle
A ball-shaped collection of chemicals in water that are both hydrophilic and hydrophobic, formed when cleaning dirt.

Monomer
The chemical building block of plastic.

Nanotechnology
Technology at the nano scale—which is measured in nanometers, or billionths of a meter—that is, things smaller than the width of your hair.

Penicillin
The first antibiotic to be used as a medicine.

Pesticide
Chemicals sprayed on crops to kill pests that eat the crops.

pH
The scale used to measure the acidity of a substance.

Polymer
A substance made of many monomers bonded together, such as plastic.

Prosthetics
Artificial body parts that are made to replace a missing part.

Surfactant
A chemical that reduces the surface tension of water.

Tissue engineering
Creating new body parts that can do the job of natural tissues, by combining cells and other biological material with physical frames.

Transplant
Replacing a diseased organ with a healthy one from another person.

Picture credits
The Publisher would like to thank the following for permission to reproduce their material.
Top = t; Bottom = b; Center = c; Left = l; Right = r
16br ManuWe/iStock Images; 19cr Scott Downing/Alamy Stock Photo; 20cl goa novi/Shutterstock; 21tr Monkey Business Images/Shutterstock, 21bl Image Source/Alamy Stock Photo; 30c Inside Creative House/iStock Images, 30br DR P. Marazzi/Science Photo Library; 31tl Nastasic/iStock Images, 31br Newscom/Alamy Stock Photo; 34c Prostock-Studio/iStock Images, 34tr RGB Ventures/SuperStock/Alamy Stock Photo, 34br People Image Studio/Shutterstock, 34bl PhotoEdit/Alamy Stock Photo; 36cl vchal/Shutterstock; 37tr vm/iStock Images, 37bl Kateryna Kon/Shutterstock

INDEX

THE AUTHOR & ILLUSTRATOR

JENNY JACOBY

Jenny writes and edits books and magazines for children. From writing science activity books to inspiring profiles, puzzles, and quizzes, she is passionate about making information fun. Jenny lives in London, England, with her family. Find out more at jennyjacoby.com.

LUNA VALENTINE

Luna Valentine is a Polish children's book illustrator living in Sheffield, England. She's inspired by science, nature, and witchcraft, and loves creating fun, lively characters who often get up to no good in their respective stories. When Luna's not drawing, it's only because one of her three pet rabbits has run off with her pencil.